MW01635395

# The Little Red Octopus Finds A Helper

*To Raquel, Kira and Summer*
*My true rainbow*

*—TP*

# The Little Red Octopus Finds A Helper

Written by Todd Peterson
Illustrated by Phil Watson

www.thelittleredoctopus.com

RAKISU PUBLISHING



ISBN-13: 978-0-9909694-1-9
LCCN: 2015910652

*Printed in the United States of America*

The Little Red Octopus was ready to eat her cake all by herself, because she had baked it all by herself.

No one had helped her when she asked.

Not the lazy Blue Turtle.

Not the fluttery pink Puffer Fish.

Not the two sneaky Green Eels.

As she nibbled the first slice, a tiny Gold Starfish tapped on her tentacle and whimpered, "Please give me one of your sparkly slices. They look so yummy and you have so many."

"You want me to give you one of my sparkly slices? Where were you when I asked, 'Who will help me make the cake?'" asked the Little Red Octopus.

"I gathered the plankton all by myself."

"I mixed the batter all by myself."

"I baked the cake all by myself."

"And I decorated it all by myself."

“So does anyone really deserve a slice of my sparkly cake?”

"But I'm SO small and I
didn't think I could help"
whimpered the tiny
Gold Starfish.

"Ohh... You can always find a way to help," proclaimed the Little Red Octopus.

"But I'm too late!  There is nothing left to do,"
whimpered the tiny Gold Starfish.

"Well I know what you can do to help AND enjoy a yummy slice of cake too," said the Little Red Octopus.

"What can I do?"
whimpered the tiny
Gold Starfish.

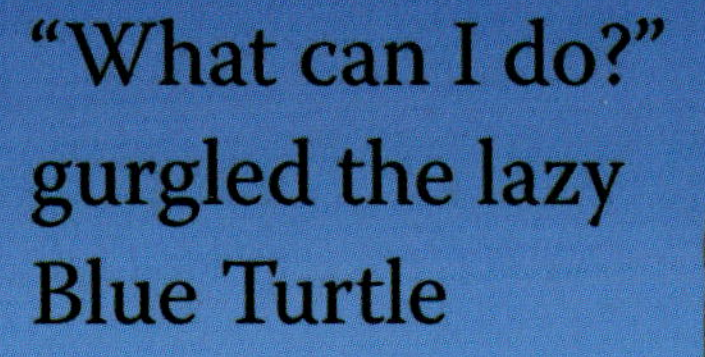
“What can I do?”
gurgled the lazy
Blue Turtle

“What can I do?”
chirped the fluttery
pink Puffer Fish

“What can we do?”
squealed the sneaky
Green eels.

“You can all clean the dishes!”
laughed the Little Red Octopus.

And so they did.

The Blue Turtle and the Gold Starfish cleaned the spoon.

The Pink Puffer fish cleaned the bowl.

The two Green Eels put them away.

And they were all very happy.

“Thank you all for helping” said the Little Red Octopus.

And that's how everyone enjoyed a slice of cake.

And that's how the
Little Red Octopus
found her little helper.